AF346266

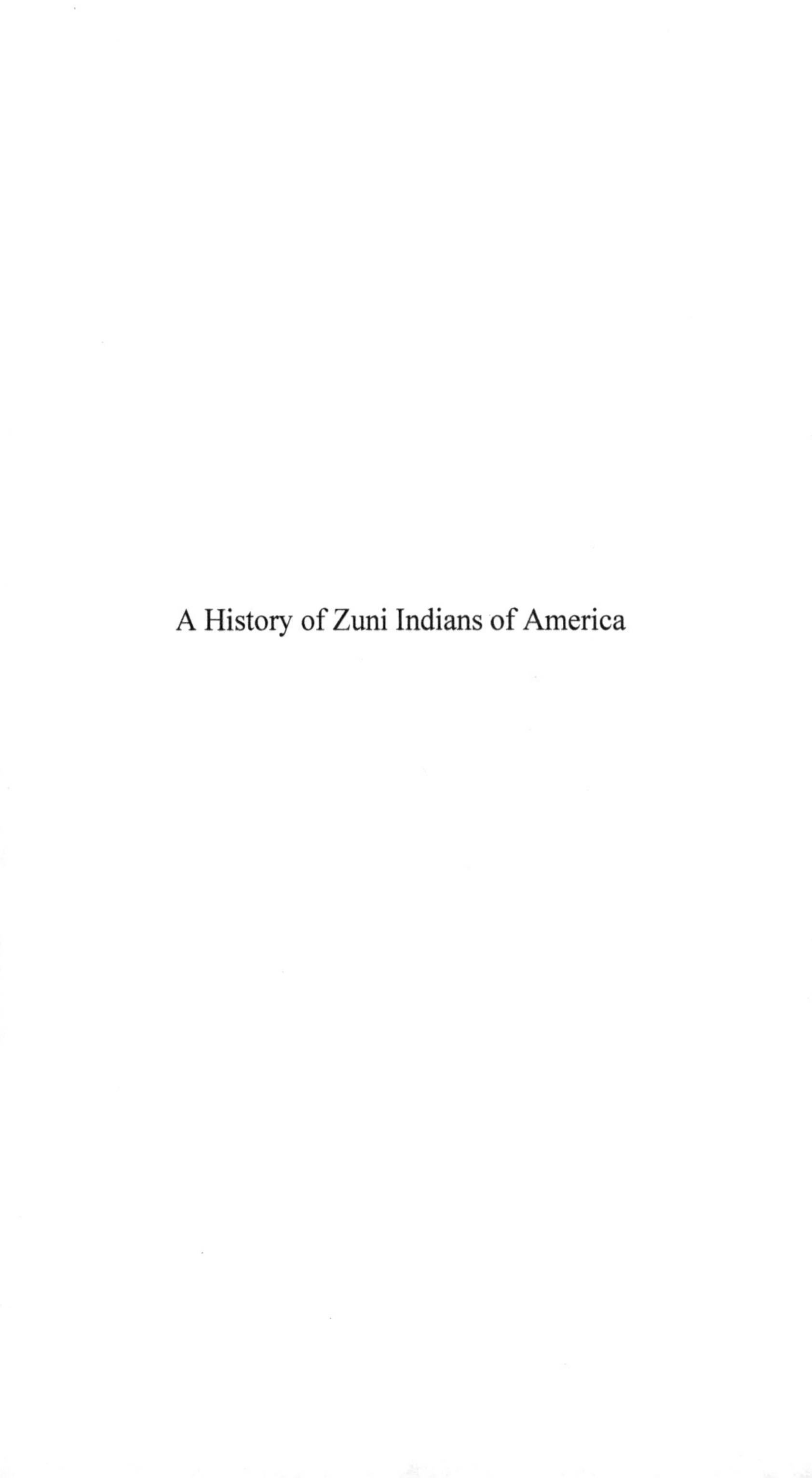

A History of Zuni Indians of America

A History of Zuni Indians of America

This collection is based on the works of:
Andrew A. MacErlean
Francis Klett
John G. Owens
Frank H. Cushing

Editions LM

History and Civilization Collection

Chapter 1

General History of Zuni Indians[1]

The Zuni Indians are Native Americans; a Pueblo tribe residing at Zuni on the bank of the Rio Zuni near the boundary of New Mexico, and in the adjoining villages of Nutria, Ojo Caliente, and Pescado.

The name Zuni is a Spanish corruption of the Keresan *Sunifisti*, and was first used by Antonio de Espajo in 1583; the natives however called themselves Ashiwi (from *Shiwi*, flesh) and their homeland Shiwinnaqin.

They were discovered by Fray Marcos de Niza, a Franciscan missionary in 1539. Fray Marcos accompanied by a black Estavanico

---

[1] Based on the work of Andrew A. MacErlean.

and some Indian guides had set out in that year to prepare the way for his fellow missionaries in unexplored regions. Estavanico had been sent forward to inspect the unknown lands; when Fray Marcos arrived in Arizona after passing through Sonora he learned that Estavanico had been killed.

Nevertheless, he continued his journey and got sight of Hawikuh, one of the seven Zuni villages or pueblos. Owing to the hostility of the inhabitants, he was forced to return to Mexico, where he published an account of his journey, relating what he had heard of the Kingdom of Civola. This glowing description of the region led to the expedition of de Coronado in 1540, the little army being accompanied by Fray Juan de Padilla.

Coronado, after storming Hawikuh, discovered that Fray Marcos had been misled by the reports of the Indians, and that Cívola's rich cities were only seven ordinary Indian *pueblos*, none containing over 500 houses. In 1598 Fray Andres Corchado was sent to preach to the Zuni and the neighbouring tribes. This first permanent mission among the former was begun at Hawikuh in 1629 by the Franciscans.

On 22 February, 1632, Fray Francisco Letrado, and, five days later, Fray Martin de Arvide were martyred by the Zuni. When the Apache attacked Hawikuh on 7 August, 1670, and destroyed the Zuni church, another Franciscan, Fray Padro de Avila y Ayala, gained a martyr's crown.

In 1680 the Zuni joined in the Pueblo rising, killed their missionary, and fled, as they usually did when stricken with fear, to their fortress of Taaiyalone. The mission was continued until the nineteenth century, when it decayed from a want of priests and resources.

The Zuni were the first of the Pueblo tribes met by the Spaniards, and have changed but little in character since that time. They were in general peaceful unless much provoked, tenacious of their traditional practices and beliefs, intellectual and serious, yet at times very witty. Their features are clear cut, noses aquiline, and lips thin; contrary to most of the Pueblo tribes very many of them are long-headed. Albinos, with light golden hair and pink-gray or blue eyes, are not unfrequently met among them.

The term Pueblo Indians (so called form the Spanish *pueblo*, a village) was applied to denote those Indian tribes living permanently in groups of adobe or stone houses in Arizona, New Mexico, and the adjoining part of Mexico, and in prehistoric times in Utah and Colorado.

In 1581 Francisco Sánchez Chamuscado and three Franciscans, Augustin Rodríguez, Francisco Lopez, and Juan de Santa Maria, were slain by the Tigua Indians near the Rio Grande. Seventeen years later Juan de Onate visited this region, and, dividing it up into districts, had each district entrusted to the care of a missionary, thus definitively bringing the Pueblo into contact with civilization; but the scarcity of priests available retarded the spread of Christian truth.

In 1630, in answer to an appeal, thirty more franciscans came to the mission and worked with great success, until August, 1680, when disputes having arisen between the civil and ecclesiastical authorities, the Indians broke into rebellion, destroyed the missions and the religious archives, and murdered twenty-one of the thirty-three Franciscans as well as several hundred colonists. Again in 1696 an insurrection occurred and some more of the friars lost their lives, but since then the Indians have in general remained tranquil, though in 1847 Governor Bent was murdered by the Taos, incited by Mexicans; on the other hand the Zuni in particular have been very friendly and faithful to the Americans, supporting them in the Mexican War.

In the northern part of the Pueblo region the village dwellings were generally constructed of sandstone or lava blocks; in the southern most of the houses were of adobe. The houses were generally several stories high, with ladders or steps on the outside, the roof of one story serving as a kind of veranda for the story above. The ground floor, evidently for reasons of defence, had no door, entrance being made by means of movable ladders. The houses were owned and built by the women, the men supplying the materials. The pottery and weaving of the Pueblo Indians are the finest in the present territory of the United States; while the basket work of the Hopi in particular is highly esteemed. The northern Pueblo were adept agriculturists, and made use of a system of irrigation. Corn and cotton were extensively grown. At present, beans, chile, melons, and pumpkins are carefully cultivated. Fish is never eaten, and there are few domesticated animals except the turkey and dog. The Pueblo men usually wore a jacket and trowsers of deerskin, though now they use woollens; the women wear a cotton shirt and a woollen blanket passing over the right and under the left shoulder, and caught at the waist with a long coloured sash.

Each tribe is formed of a certain number of clans, descent being through the maternal line; formerly the clan was presided over by a priest. The Zuni had many secret societies dealing with agriculture, magic, religion, war, etc. These societies could be entered only after severe ordeals had been successfully borne. As part of an initiation ceremony among this tribe chosen men clad only in the breech-cloth had to walk to a lake forty-five miles distant, under the blazing sun, to deposit a plume-stick and pray for rain; while one of the trials to be undergone by a candidate for admission to the priesthood of the Bow, was to sit unclad for hours on a large ant-hill.

The rituals of the Pueblo contain many prayers; thus the Zuni have prayers for food, health, and rain. Prayer-sticks, that is sticks with feathers attached as supplicatory offerings to the spirits, were largely used by the Pueblo. These sticks are usually made of cottonwood about seven inches long, and vary in shape, colour, and the feather attached, according to the nature of the petitions, and the person praying. The stick is intended to represent the god to whom the feathers convey the prayers that are breathed into the spirit of the plumes.

The Hopi had a special prayer-stick to which a small bag of sacred meal was attached. Green and blue prayer-sticks are often found in the Pueblo graves and especially in the ceremonial graves of Arizona.

Polygamy among the Indians is unknown; the woman is the more important element in married life; she has the power to divorce the husband for trifling reasons, and he then returns to his parents' home, the children, if any, belonging to the mother. In former times the government was in the hands of the Indian priests; since the

Spanish conquest, however, purely civil affairs are controlled by an elected body.

Chapter 2

Zuni Indians of New Mexico[2]

Another interesting branch of the aborigines of North America is that of the Zuni, a thriving tribe, inhabiting a remote section of the Western United States. This people belongs to the Pueblos, a semi-civilized remnant of the Aztec Empire. Their home is in an uninviting portion of the desert district of New Mexico, about 200 miles southeast of the Moquis settlements.

Leaving Fort Wingate, our route lay southwest across a luxuriant, well-timbered spur of the Zuni Mountain, and thence along the Rio Zuni, which was dry, excepting in spots. Passing Ojo de Pescado, a summer

---

[2] By Francis Klett

retreat of the Zuni, after a weary march through scorching sands, we came, on July 22d, to the suburbs of Zuni town, the outline of whose houses could be traced at a distance of more than a mile; even the characteristic ladder, extending far above the roof, being distinctly visible. As we approached, single dwellings here and there came into view, situated amid corn and water-melon fields. On coming nearer, an old church stood prominently forth, its two well-preserved bells hanging in an opening in the wall over the entrance.

Unlike the Moquis, whose settlements are on lofty rocks, the Zuni town is located on a slight rise above the level of the surrounding plain. Its area is about half a square mile, with streets running here and there at right angles. Much rubbish and *débris* are encountered in entering the town. The houses are of *adobe* terraced, well built, and principally of two—though some are of three, and not a few of even four—stories. As a means of entrance, ladders are used; although in a few cases there are ground-doors (*see* engraving), still the usual method of ingress is by ladder to the second story, thence inside by steps up and down. Some of the dwellings have isinglass windows, while the doors generally are hung on hinges. Each floor is divided into several apartments.

FIG. 1.

PUEBLO OF ZUNI.

On arriving at the town, our guide, Swzano, a Zuni, insisted on our first visit being made to himself. Climbing to the second story of his house by ladder, we scrambled in after a fashion, and were corned by himself and wife, who at once seated us comfortably on sheep-skin rugs spread on the bare earthen floor; bread and water were forthwith handed us, these constituting the simple but recognized symbol of great hospitality among this people.

After a pleasant hour in the company of our guide and his wife, we sallied forth to see the town. Coming to one of the larger houses, we gained ready admission, and were hospitably received. Our presence, however, was the occasion of much comment among the women, of whom we found six in one room. Their peculiar chattering, accompanied by hearty laughter and strange gesticulation, though unintelligible to us, was construed into joking at our expense. The men were in the field at work, while the children were enjoying a bath in the muddy waters of the Rio Zuni.

The women were engaged in grinding corn and wheat, an operation effected by means of several pairs of large, flat stones, some of coarse and others of fine material. Between the first set of stones the grain is merely mashed, each successive pair rendering the particles smaller and smaller, the last turning out fine flour. Two other women, in another room, were engaged in baking bread, which is made into thin cakes, or wafers, similar to the *marros* of the Jews, only the latter are the harder. On inspecting the house, we found each apartment whitewashed, both walls and ceiling, well ventilated, and in every respect neat and clean; exceeding good order seemed to prevail in the domestic appointments throughout the establishment. The furniture consisted of but few articles, these being principally sheep-skins, Navajo blankets, and water-vessels, the latter used also for cooking-purposes. These vessels are of their own manufacture, of burnt earth, and, in many instances, highly embellished with fanciful designs of neat pattern, the figures being either brown or black, on a ground-work of white. No beds are seen in the house, blankets alone serving as such; the occasional bird-skin, hanging by a string in some corner, serves as a charm. Live eagles and sparrow-hawks, tamed by these people, are seen about almost every house, great veneration being had for these members of the feathered tribe, which are considered the sacred birds of Montezuma. Each dwelling is provided with a loom, which forms a conspicuous part of the furniture. It consists of two sticks, between which the threads, of the width of the blanket to be made, are spread, the whole arrangement being fastened to the floor and ceiling by raw-hide strings. The operator squats on the ground, using for a shuttle a stick to which the wool for the cross-threads is fastened. The operation of weaving is skillfully performed, although a long time is required in the manufacture of one of their blankets.

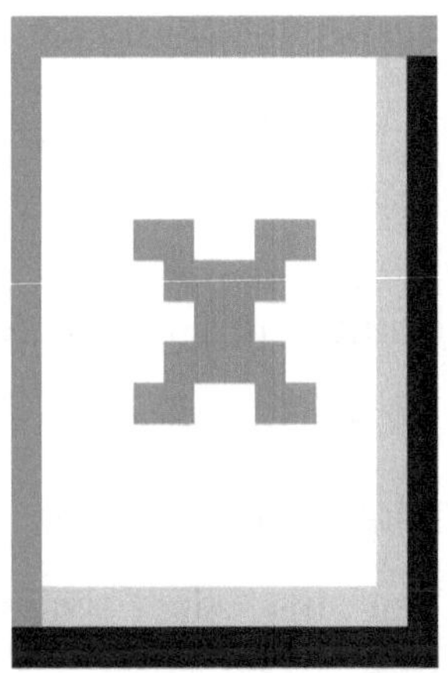

CATHOLIC CHURCH AT ZUNI.

The domestic animals of the Zuni are goats, fowl of all kinds, a few head of cattle and donkeys—every family owning several of the latter, which, while serving for transporting wood great distances, as well as for riding, are used chiefly in cultivating the fields.

One specimen among the goats had four horns, as shown in the engraving, and was said to belong to the species formerly common among the Navajos, called *cimeron*. The sheep are raised for their wool.

FIG. 3.

29

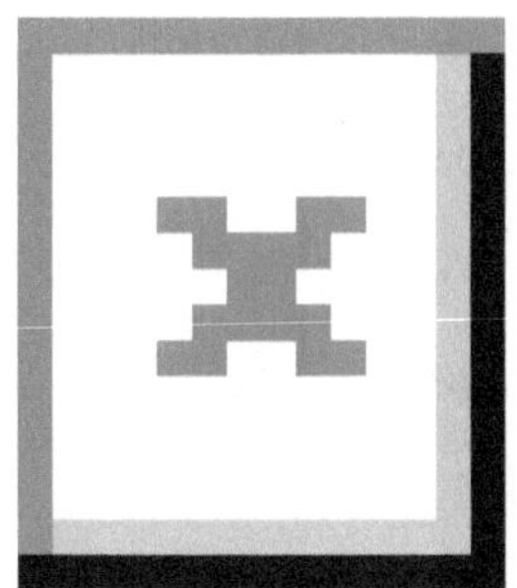

HEAD OF FOUR-HORNED SHEEP.

Outside the town there is a large farm, of which a sketch is presented. It is cultivated in common by the Zuni, although divided into patches, or small gardens, one of which belongs to each family.

No rains occurring for long periods, irrigation is resorted to, the water being supplied by the Rio Zuni, in the vicinity of the town; this water is salty. For drinking-purposes, wells are sunk at different points, good water being everywhere abundant at a moderate depth.

The staple products are wheat and corn; vegetables are raised in abundance, chiefly onions, *chile* (Spanish pepper), and caraway. From *close* conversation with the people, however, one would suppose their partiality for the first-mentioned vegetable predominated. Melons and pumpkins are also considerably cultivated.

Sauntering about the village, several underground courts were encountered, as well as subterranean passages from one square to another, and to the old Catholic church. This church is of *adobe,* and at least 200 years old; it is 120 feet long, 40 feet wide, and, within, 130 feet in height.

The altar is covered with a profusion of carving, which still shows in traces gilding and colors; it has a painted altar-piece of rude construction, representing the ascension of the Virgin Mary; here and there are carved statues of saints, while on the walls are two illegible inscriptions in Latin. In this church, we were told, a zealous priest celebrated the rites of the Romish Church for a brief period; but no

Gloria or *Te Deum* has been heard within its wall for upward of a hundred years.

The Zuni authorities are a governor and high priest; the latter is called the *cacique,* who, besides being the oracle of the tribe, is their temporal as well as spiritual ruler. No outward personification of their Divine Being is made use of; but, entering their *estufas* (temples) with a *bueno corazon* (good heart), they simply pray for some blessing, looking to no visible object as a medium of intercession between themselves and their God. Although for a time they outwardly observed the religious teachings of their conquerors, inwardly they maintained the belief of their race in the infallibility of their traditions, and soon repudiated the creed pressed upon them, returning to the worship of the source of light — the sun — as their only true God. But not only here were the Jesuits expelled; they were also driven out from the pueblos of Jemez, Acoma, and Saguna, as the ruins of the churches testify. However, at a few points the Jesuits still hold sway, as, for instance, with the Isletta Pueblos on the Rio Grande, while with the Mexicans of New Mexico the Jesuits are everywhere in full power. In times of great drought, and during festivals, the cacique orders the celebration of the *cachina*, a sacred dance.

Fortunately, it being a holiday with them at the time of our visit, the rare opportunity was afforded us of witnessing this unique, interesting, and most beautiful though heathenish custom, of which a sketch was made on the spot. Some twenty-seven persons were engaged in the ceremony.

When first seen, the participants were standing in a row, their faces toward the sun; they were gayly dressed, as will be evident from the description of the three styles of costume worn on the occasion, and represented in the engraving.

N° I. represents a dancer — costume, light-blue mask, horse-hair beard, necklace of black wool and beads, wreath of hemlock as a waistband; short white skirt, with fancy border, held at the waist by a green and black sash, to which was attached a bunch of long, white strings, hanging to the ground along the left leg; a land-turtle's shell, pendent from the left garter below the knee, contained pebbles which served a purpose similar to the castanet of the Spanish dancer; hemlock around the ankles, yellow eagle-feathers in the hair, and a fox-skin suspended from the waistband, complete the make-up.

N° II. represents the captain, who was attired thus: Yellow eagle-plumes in the hair; blue tunic, white under-garment, with fancy sidepiece inserted, and blue stockings; in one hand a staff was carried, the other holding a vessel containing flour.

N° III. represents a female dancer (character taken by male); costume, a white *serape*, with black border interwoven with fancy colors, and a blue gown; otherwise, the attire was that of N° I.

The male dancers stand in a row, the female (males assuming the character) facing them and chanting a low, solemn strain, keeping time with the right foot. In the intervals between the songs, the leader scatters flour to the four winds to appease the anger of their Divine Being, and induce him to send water from heaven. December is the period of their greatest festivity and rejoicing.

During this month their God sends his two sons, one to visit the living, the other the dead, of this "his chosen people." Their *estufas* are also used as halls for public meetings.

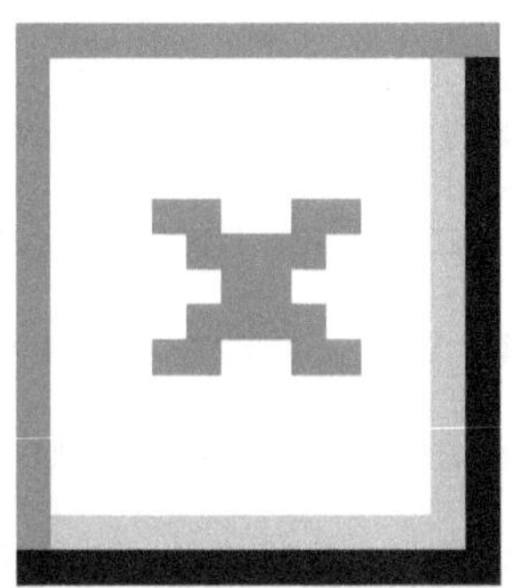

CACHINA DANCERS.

The executive authority of the Zuni is vested in an officer styled governor one—Pedro Pino—who, however, is but the mouth-piece of the spiritual ruler, the cacique; the orders of the latter are the laws governing the tribe, their execution simply resting with the governor. In conversation, Pedro Pino informed us that he was the ruler of the country between the Neutrias and Colorado Chiquito, some sixty miles, and Agua Fria and the Moquis settlements, about one hundred miles apart. In appearance, he is perhaps sixty years old, of commanding presence and affable manners; his hair is snow-white. He told us he had been governor of the Zuni people for many years, and that the tribe had always been friendly to the whites (Americans), from many of whom he had testimonials to the latter effect. Ordering his son, Patrizio, to bring him certain papers, he produced letters from officers of our army and private citizens, which referred to the governor in the highest terms, and also spoke of the uniform kindness in their treatment of his people.

"The Americans," continued the governor, "treat us well, but the Mexicans very badly; the latter have always maltreated us, and we want them neither to go through our country nor to reside among us. The heavens punish us by long drought for allowing them to remain on the Colorado Chiquito. My cacique, who prays for rain, and who is the spiritual and temporal ruler of this people, watches the sun daily, and is much distressed because no rain falls. He (the cacique) attributes the drought to the presence of the Mexican on our soil."

Pedro Pino bade us tell the Great Father that he wanted a "perpetual title to the Zuni country, which," he said, "had been handed down to us by our forefathers, through all time." Further, he remarked: "We are peaceable, and do not make war; if we have a title to our lands from the Great Father, we can show the document, and even the Mexican will respect it." The cacique, who was present, nodded assent, but did not join in the conversation.

The governor very cheerfully and politely accompanied us through the village. As the *cachina* dancers came in sight, and we halted to witness the ceremony, an elderly man approached and remonstrated with the governor for allowing us to look upon this form of worship. In reply to the remonstrance, Pedro Pino informed the intruder that he would allow us, "but," said he, "no Mexican shall ever look upon the performance of this holy and sacred rite. The Americans," he continued, "have ever been our friends, and are good and excellent people. I have been in Washington, and have seen such men as Monroe and Calhoun, and have been in the halls of Congress. These men" (pointing to us) "come from Washington, and I know they are good men." To the last remark *we* bowed assent.

On returning with the governor, we were most cordially welcomed to his house, and, entering, were very agreeably and hospitably entertained. A pipe "all round," and Pedro Pino entered into conversation.

He spoke of a single Mexican at Ojo de Benado, and another at the Colorado Chiquito, who were a sore grievance to his people. He said: "The cacique of my nation is very sorry on this account, and the rain will not fall while these wicked men inhabit our territory. I will deem it a special favor if you will intercede with the Great Father for a title for us to our country: this will satisfy us. You men are good, have seen the sacred dance of the *cachina*, and we shall have rain." It may be a fact of importance to the superstitious to know that it *did* rain that evening, and most heavily, the storm lasting several hours!

The traditions of the Zuni are few and simple. They say their people came from the northwest on their march southward; that all Pueblo Indians belong to a common race, and are all members of the large families called Aztecs, or Montezumas; that some of their forefathers remained behind in the great migration of the nation, while the large body pursued a southerly course, ultimately forming the mighty empire of Mexico, as found by Cortez after its conquest; that, long before the white man came, their people inhabited the *mesa* south of their town. They have traditions, also, of a flood; of the founding of their present *pueblo;* of their war with the Spaniards, and their subjugation, by the latter, for a time; of the arrival of the first American in New Mexico, and of the Mexican and Navajo War. But their knowledge of these events is merely outline, they being unable to give any details.

The Zuni language is much like that of other Pueblo Indians, but the words are, apparently, rather indefinite, requiring much facial contortion and bodily gesticulation to make their sentences perfectly intelligible. They have no schools. Their hieroglyphical writings may be seen in many places, while all along the Cañons de Choca and de Chelle are traces of the ancient march of this people. At Mesa Pintada (Painted Rock), about 100 miles to the northward, we copied one of their hieroglyphical inscriptions, as seen in the engraving.

This writing being in the Navajo region, is believed by some to be the work of that tribe; but this could hardly be, since the Navajoes are a nomadic people, and, besides, are not known to possess hieroglyphical writings. The Mesa Pintada is a vertical wall of sandstone, about 150 feet high. The inscription, as here given, was copied on the spot, and is a faithful representation. Commencing at *a,* the writing runs, with the mesa, westward; the space from *a* to *e* is 16 feet; the figures are reduced to one-fifth their original size.

ZUNI VEGETABLE-GARDENS.

There are many ruins of stone-houses in the vicinity of Zuni, at Agua Fria, El Moro, Ojo de Benado, and Old Zuni, which were undoubtedly towns inhabited at the time of the Spanish conquest, constituting, with Zuni, Neutrias, and Ojo de Pescado, the *Seven Cities of Cibola,* mentioned frequently by Castañede in the description of his travels in 1540. The opinion of the chief officer of this expedition, Lieutenant Wheeler, is in accordance with the views of General Simpson, Lieutenant Whipple, Mr. Gallatin, and other ethnologists. Moreover, the governor of the Zuni informed us that all the ruins in question were once thriving towns of his people. In connection herewith it may be mentioned, that near Zuni is a rock with an old Spanish inscription, which our party photographed.

GROUP OF ZUNIS.

The Zuni number about 2,000 souls. In summer, parts of the tribe resort to the smaller settlements — one at Neutrias, the other at Ojo de Pescado (respectively about twenty miles from Zuni town)—to cultivate their farms in those sections. Their fields do not compare unfavorably with those of the Mexicans.

In appearance, the Zuni are a mixture of Mongolian and Caucasian. The complexion is olive, rather than dark-brown; hair straight and jet black; eyes black; cheek-bones very high and prominent; their height and general *physique* correspond to the average among the whites.

Their dress is simple, that of the men being merely cotton drawers and shirt, with blue woolen stockings of their own manufacture; a turban of wool or cotton completes the male attire. The females wear a gown of wool, held at the waist by a sash of the same material; the arms and shoulders are left bare; their stockings same as those worn by the men; for shoes, both males and females wear moccasins of buckskin. When in the street, the women cover the head and shoulders with a white cloth.

Among the Zuni, as well as other Pueblo Indians, are many albinos, and, as interesting to those inclined to the Darwinian theory, it may be stated that the production of this "improved stock" is not due to any mixture of white blood.

The skin, and sometimes the hair, of these singular specimens of humanity, is perfectly white, while their eyes are of a reddish hue. The mother of an albino being asked why, she being *brown* her child was *white* made no reply; her fierce look, however, expressed more, perhaps, than her language would have revealed.

FIG. 7.

HIEROGLYPHICS AT MESA PINTADA.

Several tribes of Pueblo Indians have been contaminated by contact with the Spaniards, but the Zuni are still pure, and free from taint through Spanish influence. They are simple, though ceremonious in manners—the latter trait undoubtedly acquired from occasional association with their Latin conquerors.

They are extremely hospitable, and, after short acquaintance, are apt to prepossess the stranger and to command his respect. The females are chaste, reserved, extremely modest and rather shy, avoiding, when possible, the gaze of the stranger. Many of them are quite pretty, of fine figure and regular features. Their want of personal cleanliness, however, was apparent, and is certainly singular, in view of the neatness which pervades their dwellings.

One cannot but admire their regard for truth, their industry, unobtrusive disposition, hospitality and respect for strangers. Their hatred of the Mexican is intensely bitter, and is not concealed.

On every favorable occasion they give vent to expressions indicative of outraged feelings by reason of the persecutions that have been inflicted upon them by their enemies; and these, together with the feeling manner in which they are made known, warrant the belief that the injuries they have suffered have been numerous and severe. Their love for and kindness toward the people of the States (or "Americans," as they call them) are in striking contrast with the hatred and revenge they bear the Mexican. Yet the benefits they have received from our Government have been neither many nor great.

Although perhaps these Indians, like all Pueblos, do not impress the stranger very favorably on first sight, on closer acquaintance one is forced to yield to the conviction that they are among Nature's noblemen—that they are the descendants of a race long freeholders of the soil of the North American Continent, and are every way worthy of confidence and respect.

They are by no means to be compared to the nomadic tribes of red-skins, everywhere infesting the prairie, plain, and mountain of the far West, for murder and plunder. Like other Pueblo tribes, these people show marked and distinctive peculiarities, not that they differ essentially in type from the other branches of the great aboriginal families, but as regards their originality in costume, and their strong conservatism. Industrious and self-sustaining, they are temperate and quiet; though receiving but little aid from the General Government, they are well to do, and particularly in the line of farming.

As evening drew near, we prepared to bid adieu to Zuni town and its inhabitants. On leaving, the governor, with his cacique and the prominent men of his tribe, followed us to the outskirts of the village, when, with uplifted hands, he gave us his benediction, imploring the God of the Zuni to give us safe return to our camp, and, at the close of the field season, to our homes and kindred in the distant East.

A pleasant day with this isolated band of self-supporting, half-civilized people, was profitably spent, many facts being gained regarding themselves, their ancestors, their peculiar manners and customs, as well as respecting their language. These data, when properly discussed and elaborated, will constitute additional information of interest to the general reader, as well as of value to the student of ethnology and philology, and may, moreover, throw new light on the history of the North American aborigines, of whom but a handful remain to tell the story of their former greatness, or the extent of their ancient civilization.

Chapter 3

Some Games of the Zuni[3]

Play finds its best exemplification in the Indian of the South-west. Living in a mild and genial climate, naturally shiftless and improvident, this true child of Nature consumes his exuberant vitality by play instead of work. Step to the bank of the Zuni River on one of those supreme mornings in August, which only the matchless climate of New Mexico knows, and you will behold a sight which for genuine mirth and romp will surpass that of any Eastern outdoor gymnasium or children's park.

---

[3] By John G. Owens.

The river, a stream of less than ten feet, winds like a serpent through a sandy bed about one hundred feet wide. This river-bed is the chief playground of the Zuni child. Here boys and girls, some clad, some with only ear-rings or a chance necklace, are bathing, racing, wrestling, throwing sand, perchance riding some razor-backed hog; everywhere are life and merriment. I think it worthy of note that not once during the whole summer did I see a quarrel of any kind.

This spirit of playfulness remains with the boys and characterizes their later life. Not so with the girls. These, to the age of thirteen or fourteen, are very jolly and playful, but after that they begin to age very rapidly. This is probably the result of early marriage, a custom of the tribe. Zuni seems to have no class of buxom young women; the transition is from joyous, frolicsome girlhood, to sedate and sober womanhood.

But, beside these sports of childhood, there are a few games which deserve our attention. They are not limited to any age, but, so far as I know, are confined to the male sex.

Before describing these games I wish to acknowledge the kind assistance of Mr. D. D. Graham, the trader—a gentleman of culture, who has lived among the Zunis many years, and is perfectly familiar with their language. Although some of these games are seldom played in summer, yet through his co-operation I have witnessed nearly all of them.

Põ-ké-an. — This game is somewhat similar to our popular game called battledoor and shuttlecock. Green corn-husks are wrapped into a flat mass about two inches square, and on one side are placed two feathers, upright; then, using this as a shuttle-cock and the hand for a battledoor, they try how many times they can knock it into the air. Some become very skillful in this, and as they return the shuttlecock to the air they count aloud in their own language — *Tō-pa, quil-ē, hī, ă-wē-ta, ap-ti,* etc. The striking resemblance to our European game suggests a common origin, and it may easily have been introduced through contact with the Spaniards. This, however, is doubtful, and I am inclined to think that we must give the Indian the credit of inventing this game rather than borrowing it, as similarity of product by no means proves identity of origin.

Shō-wē-es-tō-pa. — The number of players is unlimited. Each one has several arrows. One throws an arrow on the ground eight or ten feet in front of him, the others follow in turn, and, should the arrow thrown by any one cross that of another at the beginning of the feathers, he takes it. The limits of success are very small, and skillful throwing is required to win the arrows of another. This game is but little played at present, and I am doubtful whether the younger men of the tribe know how to play it. José California (so named because he made a trip to California on a burro) played it for me. The decline of the game is probably due to the decline of the use of the bow and arrow, but I think it has left a descendant in

Lō-pō-chē-wā.—This is played only by the boys. Instead of arrows they use pieces of bone two or three inches long with feathers tied to them. You may see five or six boys playing this game in all parts of the pueblo at any time during the summer. They generally touch the bone to the tongue before throwing it, to make it stick. The principle of the game is the same as that of the one just described.

Than-kā-lā-wā.—This game is usually played in the spring, and resembles somewhat our game of quoits. In place of the ordinary quoit they use flat stones. Any number may take part. A small stone or even a corn-cob is set up, and on this each places his stake. To determine who shall pitch first, they all throw for some distant point. He who comes nearest to the mark chosen pitches first, and each one follows according to his throw; then the game begins. The distance pitched is nearly one hundred feet. The object is to knock over the stake or pool. If the pool is knocked over, and the stone pitched goes beyond it, it counts nothing; if just even with it, the one who pitched has another chance; if it remains behind, he takes everything, and all put up again. They count it great sport, and some become very skillful in pitching.

A-we-wō-po-pa-ne —This is played by only two persons, but each usually has several backers, and considerable betting is done. One place is designated as the stone-home. One hundred stones are placed in a row a certain distance apart. Each stone must be picked up and carried separately and placed, not thrown, in the stone-home. Another point, several miles distant, is taken, and the game is for one to run to the distant spot and return, while the other gathers up the stones. As it is a contest of speed and judgment, not chance, it becomes very exciting.

This almost inordinate desire for play, which I have claimed for the Zunis, seems not to be of recent origin. The three games, *shō-wē-es-tō-pa, shō-le-wā,* and *ti-kwa-we,* were "played by the Zunis as soon as they came out of the ground," as one expressed it. That this expression may be better understood, I will quote from Mrs. Stevenson's article on The Religious Life of a Zuni Child: "Let us follow the Zuni tradition of the ancient time, when these people first came to this world. In journeying hither they passed through four worlds, all in the interior of this, the passage-way from darkness into light being through a large reed. From the under world they were led by the two little war-gods, Ah-ai-ū-ta and Mā-ā-sē-we, twin brothers, sons of the sun, who were sent by the sun to bring these people to his presence. They reached this world in early morning, and seeing the morning star they rejoiced, and said to the war-gods, 'We see your father, of whom you have told us.' 'No,' said the gods, 'this is the warrior who comes before our father'; and when the sun rose the people fell upon the earth and bowed their heads in fear."

Shō-lē-wā.—This game was played for me by Boots and José California. They have four pieces of reed about four inches long. These are differently marked; on the concave side, painted in places, and on the convex side marked with carvings, as shown in Fig. 1. Each piece is named. The one whose concave side is entirely painted black is called *quin,* the Zuni for black; the one with one black end, *path-tō;* with two black ends, *kō-ha-kwa;* and the one with a black center, *ath-lu-a.*

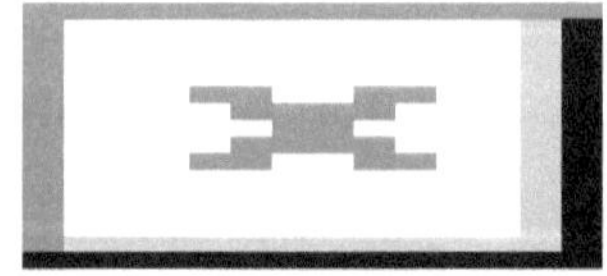

FIG. 1.—REEDS FOE PLATING SHŌ-LĒ-WĀ.

Fig. 2 shows the manner of holding these pieces when about to play. They are held in the right hand, and thrown up against a suspended blanket and allowed to fall on another blanket. Two of the pieces belong to each man and are companions. The manner in which the sticks fall determines the result. There is a pool with twelve markers in it, and he who wins the markers wins the game. The winner akes the twelve markers up into his hands and breathes on them. This is because they have been good to him and allowed him to win. It is wholly a game of chance, and horses, guns, saddles, and everything are staked upon the throw.

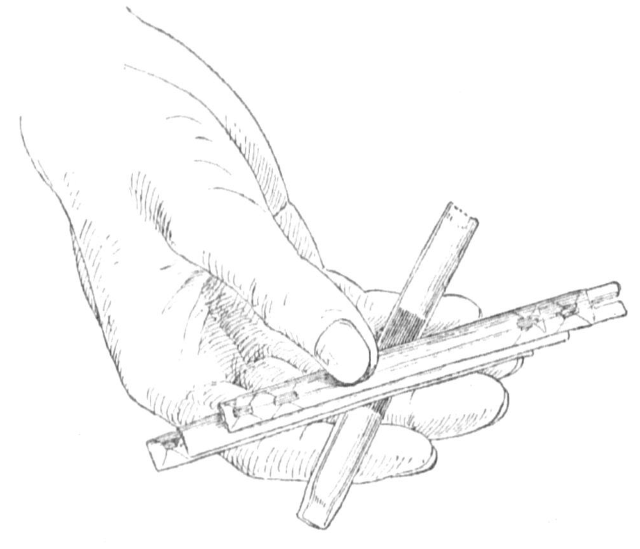

FIG. 2.—MANNER OF HOLDING THE REEDS IN SHŌ-LĒ-WĀ. T

Tash-a-lē-wā.—This is a game of chance, is played by two, and is very popular. The players sit on the ground, with a ring of forty small stones, in four sections of ten stones each, between them. The ring is usually several feet in diameter. In the center is a large flat stone called *a-rey-ley,* upon which the players make their throws. The dice, *ta-mey,* are small flat sticks about three inches long, and painted red on one side. These are taken in the right hand and thrown endwise on the central stone. If the three red sides turn up, the player scores ten and gets another throw; if the three white sides, he gets five; two red and one white, three; two white and one red, two. For counting, each player has a stick called a horse, or *touche.* Starting from the same interval in the circle of stones, each player moves his marker over as many stones as he has won points. Should the two meet at the same interval, the second one coming there will send the first one back home, and he must begin over. The idea, as given by the Indians, is, that the newcomer has dismounted or killed the first one. The horse is supposed to stop and drink at the intervals between the groups of stones. One game which I witnessed had loaded rifle-cartridges for stakes. Each player places his bet within the circle of stones.

Ti-kwa-we, or *Game of the Kicked Stick*—This is the great national game of Zuni. Among Zuni sports it ranks as baseball does among our own. It is indulged in by almost the whole male population, from boys of five or six to men of forty. Any evening of the summer one can see crowds of twenty or thirty boys skirting the southern hills and kicking the stick. Practiced thus during eight months of the year, they have an especial occasion when they contest for the championship, and this is one of the great jubilees of the tribe. Although the women do not take part, yet they show equal interest with the men and become as much excited.

The time of holding this contest is usually in the spring between the planting of the wheat and the corn. The Priest of the Bow makes six prayer-plumes and six race-sticks. The prayer plumes consist of small sticks with the white feathers from the tail of a certain species of hawk tied to one side; the race-sticks are about the size of the middle finger. The priest then takes these sticks and places them on the trail toward the south, and for four days they remain there untouched. At the end of this time he, and any others who wish to join in the race, will run out to where the sticks have been placed, and as they arrive they breathe on their hands and then kick the sticks home, making a circle of two or three miles.

Four days later a representative of each clan, each with a picture of his clan painted on his back, will run out in much the same manner. By this time most of the people have returned from their wheat-planting and the *ti-kwa-we* is in order. At present there are six *estufas* in Zuni—Ha-e-que, Ha-cher-per-que, Choo-per-que, Moo-ha-que, O-ha-que, and Uts-ann-que. The contest lies between the members of these different *estufas,* and not between the members of the different clans or parts of the pueblo, as has been stated by some writers.

Whatever *estufas* wish to contest select their men. When the men have been selected it is announced in the evening from the house-tops. This generally takes place three or four days prior to the race. This race is generally held at Zuni, but may be held at one of the farming pueblos, as Pescado, Ojo Caliente, or Nutria; in any case it is *estufa* against *estufa*. On the evening of the day before the race each side sends for a Priest of the Bow. Upon arrival he puts into the mouth of each one a piece of glass about one inch long; and with some sacred meal, taken from his pouch, he paints a mask on each one's face, then blesses them, and they repair to the hills three or four miles distant. They depart in absolute silence. Not a word may they speak unless they hear or frighten some wild animal in front of them. If the sound comes from behind, it is considered an ill omen. Having reached the hills, they dig a hole about the length of the arm and deposit in it some sacred meal, native tobacco, *hewe,* shells, and other things held valuable by the Zunis, and then retire a short distance and do not speak above a whisper. In a little while one will start for the pueblo, saying nothing, and the rest follow in single file. As they return, any manifestation of power, as thunder or lightning, is considered a good omen, as it will make them strong.

The priest who blessed them before they started awaits their return and accompanies them to the house of one of the racers or that of any member of the same *estufa.* As they reach the door of the house, those within say, "Have you come?" "We have" they reply. "Come in and sit down." The priest then blesses them, and a single cigarette is made of native tobacco and passed among the number. Then they retire for the night. Next morning everything is alive in Zuni. Indeed, for several days past the whole population has been somewhat excited over the coming event. Everyone takes sides, from the gray-haired old warrior, who believes the *ti-kwa-we* to be the greatest game ever held, to the blushing maiden whose lover is one of the contestants. Excitement runs high, and the gambling disposition of the Indian has its fullest encouragement. The small boy meets his playmate and stakes all his possessions. The veteran gambler once more tries the turn of fortune, and to counteract his heavier betting he makes a longer prayer to Ah-ai-u-ta or plants an additional plume. The contestants themselves engage in betting, and every conceivable thing of value to an Indian is either carried to the plaza, south of the old Spanish church, where it is put up against something of equal value held by an opponent, or is hurried off to the trader's store and turned into money. Ponies, sheep, goats, money, beads, bracelets, all are wagered. Sometimes also they sell the race. This is not generally admitted by the Zunis, but I have it on good authority that it has been done.

The day for the race has arrived; the runners have been up since early morning, and have taken a spin over part of the course. During the morning nearly all the members of the *estufa* drop in to tell them how much they have wagered on their success and to encourage them. About an hour before the time to start they eat a little *hewe,* or paper bread, soaked in water. *Hewe* is one of the chief breadstuffs of the Zunis, and a good *hewe*-maker is in reputation throughout the tribe as a good pastry-cook is among us. *Hewe* is made from corn batter spread with the hand on a large flat stone over a slow fire. It takes but a moment to bake it, is almost as thin as paper, very crisp, and will vary in color according to the color of the corn used. This repast of *hewe* is accompanied by a piece of humming-bird, as the flight of that bird is so very swift.

The runners then bathe in a solution made from a root called *que-me-way*. The time for the contest is at hand. The every-day attire is exchanged for the simple breech-clout. The hair is done up in a neat knot on the top of the head, and the priest pronounces a blessing as he fastens in it an arrow-point, the emblem of fleetness. He then places a pinch of ashes in front of each racer, and, standing before him, holding an eagle-wing in each hand, he first touches the ashes with the tips of the wings and then brushes the racer from head to foot. Then turning to the north he touches the wings together and says a prayer, the same to the west, south, east, the earth, and sky. I suppose the idea of the Zuni in this to be, that as he has sent a prayer to the four points of the compass, the earth, and sky, he has cut off every possible source of misfortune and danger.

Everything being now ready, the priest leads his favorites to the course across the river. Excitement in the pueblo has reached its height; the most venturesome are offering big odds in the plaza, and now all assemble to see the start.

Should a side be at all doubtful of its success in the race, an old woman is procured to sit and pray during the entire race. She sits in the middle of the room. The racers sweep the floor around her and then pile up everything that is used about the fire, such as pokers, ladles, stirring-sticks, and even the stones used to support the pots during cooking: these are to make their opponents warm; also the mullers with which they grind the corn, and the brooms: these will make them tired. A woman is chosen rather than a man, because she is not so fleet of foot. Similar ideas are found among many other peoples.

"It is a world-wide superstition that by injuring the footprints you injure the feet that made them. Thus, in Mecklenburg it is thought that if you thrust a nail into a man's footprints the man will go lame. The Australian blacks held exactly the same view. 'Seeing a Tatūngolūng very lame' says Mr. Howitt, 'I asked him what was the matter? He said, "Some fellow has put bottle in my foot."...' The Damaras of South Africa take earth from the footprints of a lion and then throw it on the tracks of an enemy, with the wish, 'May the lion kill you!'"

As each side is brought to the course the priest gives a parting blessing, and the runners take their positions opposite their opponents in single file along the course. The *tik-wa,* or stick to be kicked, is about the size of the middle finger. That belonging to one side has its ends painted red and that of the other side its center painted red, so they may be easily distinguished. The rear man of each file places the *tik-wa* across the base of his toes and sprinkles a little sacred meal upon it. Surrounding the racers will be three or four hundred mounted Indians dressed in the gayest colors. All is now ready; each rider has his eye on his favorite side, an old priest rides in advance and sprinkles sacred meal over the course, the starters kick the sticks, and the wildest excitement prevails. As each racer left his home he put into his mouth two shell beads—the one he drops as a sacrifice as he starts, the other when he has covered about one half the course. The stick is tossed rather than kicked, and a good racer will toss it from eighty to one hundred feet. Over the heads of the runners it goes and falls beyond the first man. He simply points to where it lights, and runs on.

The next man tries to kick it, but should he fail to get under it he goes on, and the next man takes it. The race is not to the swift alone, although this has much to do with it. The stick can in no case be touched with anything but the foot, and should it fall into a cactus bush, a prairie-dog hole, or an *arroyo,* much valuable time is lost in getting it out. Not infrequently it happens that one side will be several miles in advance of the other when the stick falls into some unnoticed hole. The wild and frenzied yelling which takes place as those who were behind come up and pass can only be imagined and not described. So skill in tossing it plays a prominent part. On, on they go to the southern hills, east to Ta-ai-yal-lo-ne, north to the *mesas,* follow these west for miles, then to the southern hills, and back again to the starting-point. The distance traversed is nearly twenty-five miles, and they pass over it in about two hours. Racing is indulged in by the excited horsemen as they approach the goal, and it is not unusual to see a pony drop over dead from exhaustion as they near the village. The successful runner crosses the river and runs around the heap of wagered goods near the church, then, taking up the *tik-wa* in his hands for the first time, he inhales, as he thinks, the spirit of the *tik-wa,* and thanks it for being so good to him. He then runs to his home, and, if he finds a woman awaiting him, hands the stick to her, who breathes on it twice, and he then does the same. Returning it to the woman, she places it in a basket which she has ready for it; and the next day one of the racers wraps it up with some sacred meal in a corn-husk and deposits it about six inches below the surface of the ground in an *arroyo,* where it will be washed away by the rains. Meanwhile the winners have claimed their stakes, and, should another *estufa* have a set of men to put up, the winners of the first race must compete with them until all have had a chance, and the great Zuni races are over for that year.

Kle-tak-wa (*Rabbit-hunt*).—Communal hunts seem at one time to have been held by many of the Indian tribes, and are described by the early Spaniards. Many of them were nothing less than a wholesale slaughter. Whether the Zunis ever indulged in them to that extent I am unable to say, but I saw a fence about fifteen miles to the southeast of Zuni which, I was told, extended for seventy-five miles, and was formerly used to direct the herds of antelope to a certain place.

The presence of the fence suggests the possibility that formerly such hunting expeditions may have taken place there, as Livingstone describes in southern Africa. The rabbit-hunts are described by the early Spanish chroniclers, and are still held by at least the Zunis and Moquis. Undoubtedly at one time they had a considerable religious significance, but today they have more the nature of a frolic.

The Zunis have eight rabbit-hunts a year—four by the Coyote people and four by the Eagle people. The time of holding them is fixed by the chief of the rabbit-hunts. Although held under the especial direction of particular clans, yet nearly all the male inhabitants take part. I will describe the one in which I took part last August.

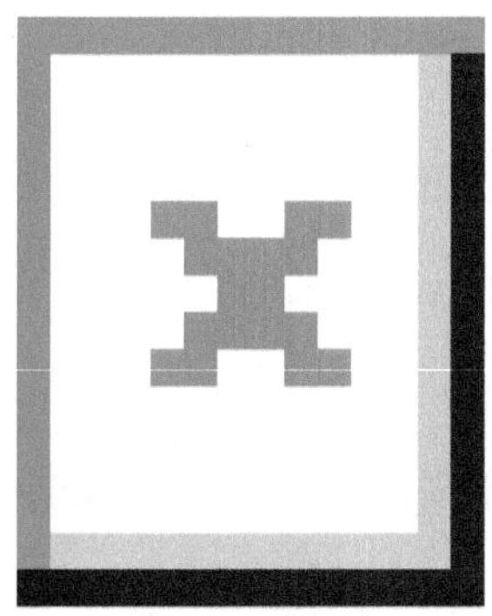

FIG. 3.—THE START FOR THE RABBIT-HUNT.

One evening about sundown I heard the herald (as is the custom of this people) announcing something from the top of the pueblo. Upon inquiry, I learned that there would be a rabbit-hunt in four days. Three evenings later, seated upon the top of the pueblo, as was our wont to do, while watching the gorgeous sunsets, we noticed that, in addition to the accustomed scene of home-returning flocks and herds, there were many herds of Indian ponies brought in and put into the *corrals*. This foretold a good turnout for the morrow. Just at nightfall the herald again proclaimed the hunt.

At noon the next day the scene in the pueblo was an active one. Everywhere ponies and horses were being saddled for the chase. Some few who had no ponies started ahead on foot. Half an hour later we all gathered on the farther side of the river, on the road to Ojo Caliente, and a picturesque crowd it was indeed—between three hundred and four hundred horsemen dressed in calico of all colors and patterns, with all kinds of head-gear, from the *sombrero* decorated with eagle-feathers to the scarlet head-band. A few had bows and arrows, others had hoes and digging-irons; but all had two or more boomerangs, called *kle-a-ne* simply curved sticks about eighteen inches long. These they use to kill the rabbits, being thrown from the horse while in motion. A few Navajoes, who also took part, added to the scene. The hunting ground was about ten miles to the southwest, on the road to Ojo Caliente. It is generally customary to have a *ti-hwa-we* on the way down. So far as I could see, no betting was done, but the excitement at times was intense. There were four racers on a side, and the course was covered in very good time.

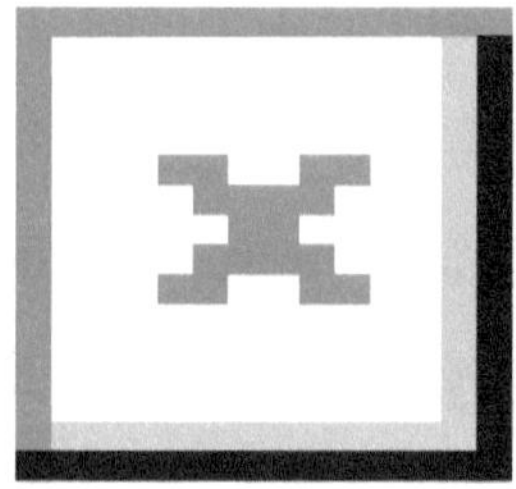

As the word was given to start, the company spread out over about an acre of ground, with the racers in the center. Each horseman cheered his side, and when the race was over I procured the *ti-kwa*. When we reached the ground, already the Cacique of the Sun had lighted a fire, and I was told he had put under it medicine to make the rabbits slow. This belief in the power to thus control wild animals is held by other peoples.

"This superstition is turned to account by hunters in many parts of the world for the purpose of running down game. Thus a German huntsman will stick a nail taken from a coffin into the fresh spoor of the animal he is hunting, believing that this will prevent the quarry from leaving the hunting ground. Australian blacks put hot embers in the tracks of the animals they are pursuing. Hottentot hunters throw into the air a handful of sand taken from the footprints of the game, believing that will bring them down."

The second priest of the Order of the Bow made a long speech, in which he told the hunters that the rabbits had been made slow, and they should get ready for the chase. After the ponies had rested a little, all mounted and set out. The more devout, however, before starting, went up near the fire, dismounted, untied their boomerangs, and got out a piece of bread. Advancing to the fire, they first said a prayer, then held their boomerangs in the flame or smoke a moment, and then threw a piece of bread into the fire as a sacrifice. Others dismounted and, without saying a prayer or offering any bread, just passed their boomerangs through the flame and remounted; while others only rode near the fire and, without dismounting, simply waved their sticks toward the flame and went on. The great majority, however, did not come near the fire at all. As I witnessed this feature of the hunt, I could not help silently observing that among the Indians there are degrees of devoutness as among white men.

The Priest of the Bow made a second and a third speech, and by this time the horsemen were well scattered over the plain. This was covered with sage-brush and scrub cedars. There are two species of rabbit, the cotton-tail (*ok-she-ko*) and the jackrabbit (*pok-ya*). There was no attempt to surround a large territory and drive the rabbits; but, as one was started up, his pursuer would give a yell, and in a few moments the harmless cottontail or jack would be surrounded by fifty or sixty horsemen. As they close in on the rabbit, those nearest it throw their boomerangs, and whoever hits it is off in a moment to claim and pick up his game. If the rabbit is not already dead, it is at once dispatched by a blow with the hand, and then it is raised to the mouth, and the hunter inhales, believing he is taking in the spirit of the rabbit. He then ties it to his saddle, and is ready for another chase. The cotton-tail often takes refuge in a hole, and then there is a grand rush to the place to reach in and pull it out. Grubbing-hoes, digging-irons, and fingers are all used to enlarge the hole, and at last the poor rabbit is pulled out, with perhaps only half his hide on. Thus it was, for three or four hours, just a succession of rallies and deploys. At the end of that time nearly everyone had one or two rabbits. Those on foot seemed to fare as well as those on horseback. I am told that sometimes they bring in wild cats and coyotes, caught in the same way, but they found none that afternoon.

About six o'clock a heavy shower came up, and the foresight of the Indian at once showed itself, for every one of them had his blanket with him, while I was thoroughly drenched. As we returned to the pueblo, many feats of horsemanship were displayed and a number of races run.

The rabbits are given by the hunters to the squaws, who place them on the floor of the house, with an ear of corn between their paws. Bandelier tells us that formerly these hunts were conducted in behalf of the caciques of the tribe, but this custom seems to have fallen into entire disuse.

Chapter 4

Story of the Zuni Social and Religious Systems[4]

The Zuni mythology, or theogony, is a reflection of Zuni sociologic or governmental institutions, with the added feature of an almost universal spiritualistic philosophy. Hence it follows that a discussion of the one must include at least a brief description of the other. Like all well-known tribes of North American Indians, the Zunis are divided into gentes, there being in their nation fifteen distinct clans or *gentes*. These again are combined into phratries, not political confederacies as among the Iroquois and Muscogee, but

---

[4] By Frank Hamilton Cushing.

ecclesiastical bands, or, in other words, into secret medicine or sacred orders, of which there are, including the wonderful and supreme organization of the Priesthood of the Bow, thirteen. Based upon this sociologic structure, the government of Zuni embraces three principles, the ecclesiastic, the martial, and the political, the outgrowths of which, in their order of precedence, are the priesthoods or caciqueships, the war chieftaincies, and the political chieftaincies. Supreme in national as well as in ecclesiastical office is the priest, or cacique of the sun, or *Pekwina,* immediately under whom are four secular as well as ecclesiastical high-priesthoods or caciqueships, the priesthood of the Pueblo, or temple of worship in—Zuni *kia kwe armosi*—with the auxiliary office *tâ shiwan okia,* or "Priestess of Seed." Selected by, yet supreme over the latter four priests in martial and secular matters, are the two high-priests, or caciques of war, who may or may not be at the same time master-priests—*Pithlan shiwan moson atchi*—of the Order of the Bow. These six priests are designated in Zuni ecclesiastical language "Priests of the Light or Day"; while resident in those special clans, which by heredity furnish the high-priesthoods (mainly the Clan of the Parrots, itself considered consanguineally descended from the gods), are numerous "Priests of the Night or Darkness," any one of whom may be chosen on the death of a priest of the light by the surviving companions. The two priests of war in turn create both the martial and political head chieftaincies, referring the.

latter to the four priests of the temple for acceptance or rejection. The martial head chieftaincy, or war chieftaincy, includes the third priesthood of the Order of the Bow, thus combining the ecclesiastical with the martial, and explaining the precedence of the latter over the political office. The third priest of the Order of the Bow, or head war-chief then names three sub-chiefs, themselves necessarily members of his own order. Likewise the head chief creates his own three sub-chieftaincies as well as the second political head-chieftaincy or chief, who in turn names his own three sub-chiefs. We find, then, that the democracy, or republic, of popular tradition, in its reference to the sedentary Indians of New Mexico and Arizona, is, like most other popular traditions regarding these comparatively unknown peoples, erroneous; that in reality their political fabric is set up and woven by an elaborate priesthood, the only semblance of democracy reposing in the power of the council—itself composed of all adults of good standing in the nation—to reject a political head chief as thus chosen, while the power of choosing a substitute remains still in the hands of the martial priests, and that of confirming him in the hands of the four priests of the temple. The latter are considered the mouth-pieces of the priest of the sun, just as the two priests of war are considered at once the mouth-pieces and, in martial and political affairs, the commanders of the four priests of the temple; and, again, the third priest of war, or head war-chief, and the first political chief, brothers to one another, yet differentiated in their functions, are considered to be the mouth-pieces of the two priests of war, the one in times of national disturbance, the other in times of peace. And yet, again, the sub-chiefs of the war-chief, as well as those of the two political head chiefs, are considered the mouth-pieces of their respective superiors.

Now, the organization of each one of the sacred or medicine orders of Zuni, less in importance than the order of the priesthood of the bow, is a miniature representation of the national ecclesiastical and martial organizations—that is, each order has its *pekwina,* or high-priest, its four *kia kwe armosi,* or priests of the temple, its two *pithlan shiwan mosun atchi,* or priests of the bow, and in accordance with its special office its medicine or prayer-priest or master, and its sacred council. Less strictly secret, yet more sacred, and organized upon similar though more elaborate principles of office, is the church of Zuni, the order of the sacred dances, or the *kâ kâ,* which is lodged in six places of worship—the half-underground *estufas* of the north, west, south, and east, the upper and lower regions of the universe. While the *kâ kâ,* as a whole, has its supreme high-priests, its priests of the temple, its warrior-priests, and its prayer-masters, each one of these six temples of worship has also its like special system of priesthood, with the added offices of song-priests or masters. Both in its organization as a whole and in its lesser organizations, the *kâ kâ* seems to be a perfect mirror, as it were, of the mythology of the Zuni nation, just as the mythology is a reflection of the sociologic organization of the same nation. It is, then, to a study of the organization and functions of the *kâ kâ,* based upon a knowledge of the national sociologic organization, that we are to look for the most complete and clear exemplification of their system of gods, just as we are to look to the traditional rituals, prayers, songs, and sacred epics of this *kâ kâ* for a comprehensive idea of their mythology. Knowledge gained from both these sources may in turn be vastly added to, strengthened, and corrected by a close study of their most abundant and beautifully imaginative folklore.

Supreme over all the gods of Zuni is *Hano ona wilona,* or holder of the roads of light, corresponding to the earthly *pekwina,* or priest of the sun, and represented by the sun itself. Beneath him is a long line of gods so numerous that I know not half their names, nor have I recorded them, but they are divided into six great classes: the celestial or hero gods (the demon-gods themselves perhaps the vestiges of a more ancient hero-god mythology), the elemental gods, or the gods of the forces of nature, the sacred animal gods, or the *kia pin* a *hâi* and *kia she ma a hâi,* the gods of prey or *wemar* a *hâi,* and the tutelary gods, or divinities of places. While *Hano ona wilona* is supreme over all, he himself, like the earthly sun-priest, is limited by his own high-priests among the gods—the celestial or hero gods, and they, in turn, by the demon-gods, while the two earthly offices of head political and war chiefs are represented, on the one hand, by the *raw* or water-wantings beings, or animal gods; and, on the other, by the *wemâr* a *hâi,* or gods of prey, while the priests of the night in the human organization (*tkwi-na-proa-a   shi-wa-ni*) seem to be represented by the tutelar gods of the deistic organization. Not less important, then, because they are supposed to act in connection with the latter, are the ancients, or spirits of the ancestors, who form the body-politic of this great system of gods, and are supposed to serve as mediators between the mortals and the gods. In Zuni belief they have also a definite place of residence assigned to them, notwithstanding which they are supposed to hold constant communion, even to the extent of occasional materialization with those whom they have left behind, to listen attentively to their prayers, and to represent them in some vague way to the higher gods of the Zuni mythology.

While this great system of gods, like the *kâ kâ,* is organized, as a whole, not unlike the ecclesiastical and martial systems of the Zunis, so also has each one of the six systems of gods, like each of the six *estufas* of the Zunis, its offices of high-priests, priests of the house or temple, warrior-priests, etc. As an example of this special organization, let me speak of the gods of the ocean, who under specific names and attributes are further distinguished as "our beloved *Pe kwi we,* or sun-priest of the ocean; our beloved the *ona ya na k'ia a shi tea ni,* or priests of the temples of the ocean; our beloved mother, the *K'o hak o k'ia,* or the goddess of the white shells; our beloved, the three great warrior-priests of the ocean, *kia chla wa ni, ku pish tai a,* and *tsi k'ia hâi a,* in whom we do not fail to recognize the two master-priests of the bow, and the third priests of the bow, or head warrior-chief of the martial organization. The lesser personages of Zuni government are finally represented by the sacred animal gods of the ocean.

Let me give, as illustrations of the deistic conceptions of the Zunis, without special reference to their rank in this governmental system of the gods, the names and supposed attributes of a few of the principal gods of Zuni mythology. *Hâno ona wilona,* or the "holder of the roads of our lives," the supreme priest-god of Zuni mythology, is supposed to hold as in his hands the roads of the lives of his human subjects, is believed to be able (to use the language of a Zuni) to see (or perceive) not only the visible actions of men, but their thoughts, their prayers, their songs and ceremonials, to will through his lesser deities whether a thing shall be or shall not be in the course of a human life. I once asked a priest in Zuni, who was about to go forth on a hunt, "Do you think you will lay low a deer this day?" and he said, "*Oothlat hâno ona wilona*" (as wills or says the holder of the roads of life). Immediately below *Hâno ona wilona* are the gods *Ahai in ta* and *Ma 'tsai le ma,* the two great deities of the priesthood of the bow, anciently known as *Ua nam atch pi ah ko'a,* the beloved both who fell (for the salvation of mankind). They are supposed to be twin children of the sun, *Hâno ona wilona*—mortal, yet divine. They were the guiders of mankind from the four great wombs of earth, the birth-place of the human family, far eastward toward the middle of the world; but, on reaching the eastern portion of Arizona, in the great exodus of the Pueblo races, they are supposed to have been changed by the will of their grandfathers— four great demon-gods—into warriors, and ever since have been the great gods of the order of the priesthood of the bow, and the rulers of the mountain-passes, and enemies of the world. Just so the young man, in modern Zuni life, who lives for years in peaceful industrial pursuits, and all at once becomes chosen as a proper person for membership in the Order of the Bow, is induced to take a scalp, and henceforth becomes a ruler of his people and his world, a warrior and a member of that most powerful of priesthoods. These two gods are supposed to have been the immediate ancestors of the two lines of priests who are now their representatives, the high-priests of the Order of the Bow; from them, in one unbroken line, has been breathed the breath of *sa wa nikia,* or the medicine of war, from one to the other of the members of their household, the *a si schlan shi we ni,* or their children, the priests of the bow, just as has been in the belief of the Roman Catholics the unbroken apostolic succession. Through their wills over the *kia sin a hai,* or annual gods, with the consent of *Hâno ona wilona,* or the "holder of the roads of life," are the roads of man's life divided, or the light of his life cut off—figurative expressions for death in the highly poetic language of the Zunis. Prior to their creation war seems to have been a secondary element in the existence of the Pueblo race; such as it previously was, however, it was represented by the great ancient god of war, the hero of hundreds of folk-lore stories, *Atchi a la to sa,* or "he of the knife-feathered wings." He is supposed to carry ever about him his many-colored bow, *a ni 'to lan,* or the goddess of the rainbow, to walk upon his swift arrow, *wi lo lo a'te,* turquoise-pointed god of lightning, and to be guarded on the right and the left by his warriors, the mountain-lion of the North and the mountain-lion of the West.

Among other beings of ancient Zuni mythology we have the marvelous example of *Oohe pololon,* or "the god of the north wind," whose breath sends the cold winds from the north region and drives the sands of the southwestern deserts, which have been stirred up by the will of the gods of the mountain. Dark and gloomy, like the clouds of the north-land home, ferocious with his shining teeth and glaring pendant eyeballs, wild with his iron-gray halo of ever-waving hair and beard, *Oohe pololon* is one of the most terrific of Zuni demon-gods. Then we have the gentle moon, mother of the women of men, through whose will are born the children of women, the representative in this system of deities of the *Shewan okao,* or seed-priestess, younger sister of the priests of the temple; and the sister of the moon, the beautiful goddess of the ocean, through whose ministrations are awakened the loves of the Zuni youth, and the good fortune of trade is secured.

While those gods in Zuni mythology remaining unknown to me are legion, yet I might continue for hours to mention gods and their attributes; as for instance, "he who carries the clouds from the ocean of sunrise to the ocean of sunset and scatters them through the heavens between"; *Kwe le le,* or "he who infuses the roots of all trees with the spirit of fire, and swings his torch in mid-air, and it forthwith bursts into flames"; *Te sha mink'ia,* or "he who dwells in the cañons and cliffs of the mountains, ever echoing the cries of his children, men and beasts of mortality."

Interesting among the hero-gods is the great priest of all religious orders save that of the bow, *Poskai ank'ia.* In the days of the new, yet not until after men had begun their journey toward the east, he is supposed to have appeared among the ancestors of the Zunis, the Taos, the Coconinos, and the

Moqui Indians, so poor and ill-clad as to have been ridiculed by mankind. He it was who taught the fathers of the Zunis their architecture and their arts, their agriculture and their system of worship, by plume and painted stick; but, driven to desperation by the ingratitude of his children, he vanished beneath the world, never to return to the abodes of men—yet he still sits in the city of the sun, ever listening to the prayers of his ungrateful children.

Let me add one more example: that of *Kia nis ti pi,* or "the great water-skate," who with his long legs measured the extent of the earth as with a compass, and between the oceans of sunrise and sunset determined the center of the world as the home of the Zunis. He is represented by a peculiar figure, and this introduces us to a new department of the subject—the conventional system of pictographs whereby the Zuni sacred orders illustrate their mythological ideas. It is first to a close study of the mythology and theogony of the Zunis, and then to that of the conventional forms of art among these and kindred peoples, that we are to look for the key to the mysterious and unnumbered pictographs of the great Southwest.

Interesting for comparison with Eastern mythology is the study of the phallic and the serpent symbolism as they occur in highly developed forms among the Zuni Indians. Yet, again, interesting because of the light that it throws upon the development of human religions and mythologies is the study of the influence of environment, physical, biologic, and sociologic, as exemplified by the religion and mythology of the Zunis.

I regret most deeply that in the limited time allowed me today I can not go into a discussion of these various questions, and into a production of the hundreds of facts illustrative of them which I have in my possession; but that I have time only to add that, as further illustrative of the connection between the Zuni sociologic and the Zuni mythologic systems is the fact that no general names for chiefs of all the departments—ecclesiastical, martial, and political—are to be found in their language, nor is there a general name for their god-priests, hero, demon, animal, elemental, celestial, or tutelar. Yet the term *awa nu thla* includes the political and martial chiefs in Zuni government, just as does the name

k'ia pin a hâ i include their representatives,
the sacred water and prey-gods, of Zuni
mythology.

www.ingramcontent.com/pod-product-compliance
Lightning Source LLC
LaVergne TN
LVHW091720190726
843493LV00001B/383